KV-451-392

CONTENTS

SYMBOLS KEY

The following symbols are used throughout this book:

ⓐ address ☏ telephone ⓕ fax ⓦ website address ⓔ email
ⓛ opening times ⓝ public transport connections ⓘ important

The following symbols are used on the maps:

𝒊	information office	○	city
✉	post office	○	large town
✚	hospital	○	small town
🛡	police station	=	motorway
🚌	bus station	—	main road
🚆	railway station		minor road
✝	cathedral/church	—	railway
▪	POI (point of interest)		
❶	numbers denote featured cafés, restaurants & venues		

PRICE CATEGORIES

The ratings below indicate average price rates for a double room per night, including breakfast:

£ under £100 ££ £100–200 £££ over £200

The typical cost for a three-course meal, without drinks, is as follows:

£ under £15 ££ £15–30 £££ over £30

❍ *Oxford, the city of dreaming spires*

INTRODUCING
Oxford

Introduction

'In Oxford you may see it all – century by century or face by face. She is an England in miniature; an essence of England' wrote historian and Oxford graduate Jan Morris, and it is true – there is so much to see in this pint-sized city, it's hard to know where to start. The oldest university in the English-speaking world dominates the centre and provides a wealth of historical and academic brilliance within its honey-coloured colleges. Add to this a clutch of world-class museums and galleries, and it soon becomes apparent that Oxford is a city of enviable fortune.

Architecturally, too, Oxford is a city of superlatives with such treasures as the Radcliffe Camera (Britain's first circular library) and the Sheldonian Theatre, designed by Sir Christopher Wren when he was Professor of Astronomy here. Gaze skyward to admire the fabled skyline of this grandiose city of spires. Most of the Gothic towers and steeples belong to the university – a tangle of 38 colleges dotted across the city, intermingled with shops and offices. Oxford doesn't flaunt its treasures; rather, they are hidden away through arched doorways, behind ancient stone walls and down narrow medieval alleyways, offering tantalising glimpses to the passer-by. Several of the colleges are open to the public, providing a privileged glimpse of student life. Each has an almost ecclesiastical feel with beautiful ancient buildings, impressive chapels, dining halls and libraries clustered around peaceful, grassy quadrangles. Many boast an abundance of greenery, with immaculate gardens, extensive meadows and fine riverside walks, which create a country feel.

Located at the rural heart of Middle England, Oxford is squeezed between the upper River Thames (known here as the 'Isis', from its Latin name 'Tamesis') and the Cherwell tributary. A compact city, it is easily explored on foot; however, the ultimate way to capture its essence is by boat. Hire a punt at Magdalen Bridge and drift downstream in true *Brideshead* fashion – with a picnic hamper, strawberries and champagne. In the immortal words of poet Matthew Arnold, there is probably no more pleasurable way to appreciate 'that sweet city with her dreaming spires'.

◉ *Exeter College's quadrangle is an oasis of calm*

When to go

SEASONS & CLIMATE

Oxford is popular year-round. Easter is especially lovely, with its mild spring days and water meadows ablaze with wild flowers. However, the best time to visit is April to September, when the weather is warm (mean maximum 21°C/70°F), boating is in full swing and street life is at its most vibrant. October to February is the wettest, coldest time (rarely below 0°C/32°F). Nonetheless, Christmas is a popular time to visit, when the city is abuzz with festive shoppers and revellers.

ANNUAL EVENTS

Here are some highlights of a busy calendar of events.

In February, the rowing season begins with the **Torpids** – highly spirited 'bumps' races on the River Isis – an inter-collegiate knockout competition where crews try to bump the boat ahead while avoiding being bumped by the boat behind. In late March, Christ Church **Oxford Literary Festival** (ⓦ www.oxfordliteraryfestival.co.uk) draws the crème de la crème to readings and workshops.

May Day morning is marked by Magdalen choristers singing madrigals to usher in the spring from atop the church tower at 06.00, followed by bell ringing, morris dancing and general revelry, usually in close proximity to a pub. Also in May, **Eights Week** is a second series of 'bumps' races, with the winning college declared 'Head of the River'.

The **Encaenia** takes place in June, when the Chancellor of the university leads dignitaries and dons in fine scarlet and pink gowns through the city to the Sheldonian Theatre to present honorary degrees. **Sheriff's Races** (flat-races for amateur horse riders) have taken place at Port Meadow each July since the 17th century. In August, there is **Jazz in the Park** at South Parks, and the **Oxford City Royal Regatta** on the Thames. September's **St Giles' Fair** – a street funfair – dates back to 1625, and **Christmas** is fêted by carol concerts, and morris dancing at Headington Quarry on Boxing Day.

⬤ *Postcard capturing a quintessential Oxford sight*

History

Oxford's foundations are somewhat hazy, although there is archaeological evidence that there was a religious settlement here as early as the 8th century, on the site now occupied by Christ Church. Very early Oxford seems to have been an oxen grazing ground, hence the name – derived from 'Oxen-ford'. It is thought that Saxons founded the first town here around 912, based on a Roman model. Thereafter it grew in prominence as a

◐ *Christ Church now occupies the site of ancient Oxford*

major road and river crossing, eventually becoming a thriving medieval city and the centre of the Cotswold wool industry. Oxford became a city and the centre of a diocese in 1545. For a while in the 17th century, it even served as a second capital of England, when Charles I moved his court here for three years to fight Cromwell and his Parliament, having been driven from London. In World War II, Oxford's beauty and academic reputation saved it from German bombing, as Hitler planned to make it the headquarters for his occupation of England.

Nobody knows exactly how or when Oxford's fabled university began. It is thought that the first centres of learning were monasteries established by the Augustinians during the 11th century to educate church clerics. A century later, academic Oxford had achieved European fame and had around 1,500 students. As its reputation spread, colonies of masters and students gravitated here, gradually evolving their own guilds and founding halls of residence until, by the end of the 12th century, it had become a *universitas magistrorum et scholarium*.

As early as the 13th century, the influx of scholars caused considerable strains on the local community – not just envy at their privileged positions of learning, but the effects of land taken over from townsfolk as colleges expanded. This led to extensive poverty, compounded by the Black Death in 1349, which wiped out a third of the population. Centuries on, this 'town versus gown' friction remains to some extent. With a population of only 165,000, the city receives an influx of around 20,000 students during term time – plus 3.5 million visitors annually, making tourism Oxford's second industry after education.

Culture

Oxford has long been a centre of culture and learning. Although quintessentially a university town, there's much more to see than mortar boards and graduation gowns. Over the centuries, the city has built up a remarkable array of treasures, and no stay is complete without a visit to its dazzling museums, from the world-acclaimed Ashmolean and Pitt Rivers Museums to the lesser known Museum of Oxford, with its historical overview of both town and gown.

Oxford wears its history on its sleeve, and many periods are illustrated in its streets, colleges and chapels, each with an eclectic mix of architecture. Discover many hidden gems on a Tourist Information Centre guided walk, covering such themes as the 'University and City', 'Gargoyles and Grotesques', 'Tudor Oxford' and 'The Civil War'.

The city enjoys a rich musical heritage and visitors can enjoy a programme of concerts, recitals and festivals – from classical to jazz – throughout the year, as well as attending evensong at some of the college chapels. Some of the best theatre productions outside London range from mainstream to avant-garde.

◐ *Bicycles are ubiquitous*

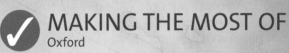

MAKING THE MOST OF
Oxford

Shopping

Oxford offers a wealth of shopping opportunities. Indeed, over the years the city has given its name to a number of products, including Oxford bags (men's trousers, fashionable in the early 20th century), Oxford shoes and Oxford marmalade.

Fortunately, the number of chain stores has been restricted on the historic High Street, making browsing its glitzy boutiques with high-end specialist shops a pleasure. The more typical high-street chains can be found near Carfax, on the two main shopping boulevards – Cornmarket and Queen Streets – and in the **Westgate Shopping Centre** (ⓐ 37 Westgate Galleries ⓣ 01865 725455 ⓦ www.westgateoxford.co.uk ⓛ 09.00–17.00 Mon–Sat, 11.00–17.00 Sun) at the western end of Queen Street. Other indoor shopping centres include the more upmarket **Clarendon Shopping Centre** (ⓐ 52 Cornmarket Street ⓣ 01865 251493 ⓦ www.clarendoncentre.co.uk ⓛ 08.30–18.00 Mon–Sat, 10.30–17.00 Sun) between Queen and Cornmarket Streets, and the tiny **Golden Cross Arcade**, with its jewellery and craft shops just off the High Street. Nearby, **Broad Street** is lined with bookshops (including several of the city's famous Blackwell stores), college gift shops and Oxford's only independent department store, **Boswells** (ⓐ 1–4 Broad Street ⓣ 01865 241244 ⓛ 09.30–18.00 Mon–Fri, 09.00–18.00 Sat, 11.00–17.00 Sun).

Off the main drags, a plentiful supply of independent gift stores, curiosity shops and quirky student-y shops offer such eclectic souvenirs as embroidered university clothing, *Alice in Wonderland* memorabilia, second-hand books and antique prints of the region.

Oxford's shopping highlight is the **Covered Market** (Ⓦ www.oxford-covered-market.co.uk), a jumble of cheesemongers, butchers, bakers and greengrocers squeezed between old-style cafés, gift shops and niche boutiques. **Gloucester Green** stages an open-air produce market (🕐 Wed morning); an antiques and bric-a-brac market (🕐 08.00–16.00 Thur); and a farmers' market (🕐 first and third Thur each month), selling an array of local produce from fruit and vegetables, to breads, cheeses and honey.

🔺 *One of the many unique shops in the Covered Market*

Eating & drinking

Oxford has a huge choice of places to eat and drink, from simple cafés and traditional pubs to trendy bistros, wine bars and gourmet restaurants.

⬤ *Stop for a bite to eat in one of the city's many cafés*

Start the day the traditional way with a hearty cooked breakfast in a simple café, where market men, suited office workers, tourists and bleary-eyed students rub shoulders over a 'fry-up' of bacon, sausage, tomato, mushrooms, black pudding, fried egg and baked beans. Two top breakfast venues are Browns and Georgina's, both in the Covered Market.

Throughout the city, coffee shops abound – even in some of the bookshops – and are ideal for a light snack or a refuelling shot of caffeine in the midst of a busy day of sightseeing. For those on the go, there are plenty of takeaway sandwich bars – or purchase picnic fare at the Covered Market for a picnic at Christ Church Meadow or while punting on the river.

Lunch is the main meal; it suits student budgets better than dinner, and there is a dazzling choice of venues catering for a mixed clientele of students, dons, locals and tourists. Most offer excellent value set lunch-menus. Many of the city's numerous pubs serve simple, reasonably priced 'pub grub' – reliable, traditional British fare – washed down with fine local beers and ales.

Afternoon tea (typically 15.00–17.00) is a curiously British ritual, with traditional cream teas (with scones, jam, clotted cream and often champagne) served in such grand venues as the Randolph Hotel. In the evening, visitors are spoilt for choice of cuisine – with restaurants ranging from Japanese to Jamaican, from Turkish to Thai, and from Mongolian to Moroccan. Many restaurants are concentrated on the High Street, Walton Street and George Street and, for a more eclectic, multi-ethnic choice, just outside the city centre on the Cowley Road.

Entertainment

Oxford offers a vast array of entertainment, ranging from choral evensong to full-scale rock concerts, and from first-class theatre to bawdy student 'fringe' events.

The student plays from the **Oxford University Dramatic Society** (ⓦ www.ouds.org) set an exceptionally high theatrical standard. Famous past members to have trodden the boards here include Richard Burton, Sir John Gielgud, Dudley Moore, Rowan Atkinson and Hugh Grant. As a result, Oxford boasts a flourishing theatre scene, with plays ranging from the mainstream to the more avant-garde and, in summer, open-air performances by the **Oxford Shakespeare Company** (ⓦ www.oxfordshakespearecompany.co.uk) in college gardens.

Classical music also thrives in such a cultural setting, with an extensive programme of amateur and professional concerts and recitals at such grand venues as the Sheldonian Theatre and the historic Holywell Music Room, which dates from 1748. During term time, there are frequent recitals in college chapels, and visitors are welcome to attend choral evensong in the beautiful chapels of Magdalen (ⓒ 18.00 daily), Christ Church (ⓒ 18.05 Mon–Sat) and New College (ⓒ 18.15 Thur–Tues). In summer, the **City of Oxford Orchestra** (ⓦ www.cityofoxfordorchestra.co.uk) performs two concert series: the 'Summer Proms' and 'Beautiful Music in Beautiful Places'.

As well as theatre and classical music, Oxford's wide-ranging cinema appeals to both blockbuster fans and art-house diehards. Nightclubs peppered about the city play music to suit all dance tastes and several bars, clubs and pubs offer a medley of live music from jazz to reggae and rock. The main venue (and launching pad for local bands Radiohead and Supergrass) is the O2 Academy.

For details of what's on when, check the free monthly listings magazine *In Oxford* (ⓦ www.inoxfordmag.co.uk) or ⓦ www.dailyinfo.co.uk – the city's most popular online listings guide. Other useful websites include ⓦ www.musicatoxford.com for classical music and ⓦ www.oxfordbands.co.uk or ⓦ http://nightshift.oxfordmusic.net for comprehensive gig listings.

🔺 The 'Bearded Ones' outside the Sheldonian Theatre

Sport & relaxation

With two rivers, a canal and the vast grassy expanses of its many parks and river meadows, Oxford lends itself easily to a variety of sports and outdoor pursuits.

Many are centred on or around water and range from pleasure cruising to towpath hikes (the Thames Towpath stretches 180 km (112 miles) from here to London). **Oxford Water Walks** (① 01865 798254 ⓦ www.oxfordwaterwalks.co.uk) offers historical and literary guided walks along the Thames and the Oxford Canal. **Salters Steamers** (ⓐ Folly Bridge ① 01865 243421 ⓦ www.salterssteamers.co.uk) passenger boats ply between Oxford and Abingdon, Henley and Windsor (May–Sept), and offer frequent, short sightseeing trips from Folly Bridge to Iffley Lock. The most quintessential Oxford experience is undoubtedly punting. Punts can be hired (🕐 10.00–dusk daily (mid-Mar–mid-Oct)) from Salters Steamers at Folly Bridge, Magdalen Bridge Boathouse (① 01865 202643 ⓦ www.oxfordpunting.co.uk) or the **Cherwell Boathouse** (① 01865 515978 ⓦ www.cherwellboathouse.co.uk).

On dry land, there is bowling at **Bowlplex** (ⓐ Grenoble Road ① 01865 714100 ⓦ www.bowlplex.co.uk), ice skating at **Oxford Ice Rink** (ⓐ Oxpens Road ① 0844 893 3222), golf at **Hinksey Heights** (ⓦ www.oxford-golf.co.uk) or **North Oxford Golf Club** (ⓦ www.nogc.co.uk), or gentle 3-hour guided cycle rides (10.00 Sat morning (summer)) run by **Capital Sport** (① 01296 631671 ⓦ www.capital-sport.co.uk). For bird's eye views of the dreaming spires, the **Oxford Balloon Company** (① 01235 537429 ⓦ www.oxfordballoon.co.uk ⓔ flights@oxfordballoon.com

⏱ Feb–end Oct) offers flights from various locations in the city.

There are also plenty of spectator sports on offer in the city. **Oxford Harlequins**, the city's premier rugby team, play alternative Saturdays at Horspath Ground (ⓐ North Hinksey ⓦ www.oxfordharlequins.com). **Oxford Cricket Club** play home league matches at Rover Sports and Social Club (ⓐ Roman Way ⓦ www.oxfordcricketclub.com). On the Thames, you can watch the rowing eights skimming the river in training for the famous Oxford versus Cambridge **University Boat Race**, which takes place in London each March (ⓦ www.theboatrace.org).

⬥ A college crew on a training outing

Accommodation

Oxford has surprisingly few hotels for such a major tourist destination so booking ahead is imperative, especially during the summer months. Accommodation ranges from cutting-edge boutique and traditional grand hotels to homely bed and breakfasts and humble pub rooms. Few offer parking facilities. For those that do, booking is essential. The range of places to stay listed below have no parking unless otherwise mentioned.

The **Oxford Information Centre** offers a booking service for hotels, hostels, bed and breakfasts, camping and self-catering accommodation (❶ 01865 252200 ❶ 01865 240261 ⓦ www.visitoxford.org/stay.asp). Outside term time, some of the famous colleges open their doors to the public (ⓦ www.oxfordrooms.co.uk), providing cheap, central accommodation within the hallowed quadrangles of a number of colleges (including Balliol, Jesus, Keble and Trinity).

Head of the River £ Clean, comfortable bed and breakfast accommodation above a popular pub by the Folly Bridge. Ask for a room overlooking the river. ❸ Folly Bridge ❶ 01865 721600 ⓦ www.fullershotels.com ❹ headoftheriver@fullers.co.uk

Oxford Camping and Caravan Club £ The closest campsite is 1.6 km (1 mile) south of the city, with basic facilities. ❸ 426 Abingdon Road ❶ 01865 244088 ❹ All year ❹ Bus: 300 (stop: Redbridge Park & Ride) ❶ Free parking

Oxford Youth Hostel £ Clean, comfortable budget rooms in a purpose-built residence, just 5 minutes' walk from the city centre. Full disabled access. ⓐ 2A Botley Road ⓣ 0870 770 5970 ⓦ www.yha.org.uk ⓔ oxford@yha.org.uk

University Club £ Although primarily a base for visiting academics and alumni, the rather institutional rooms here are open to visitors. ⓐ 11 Mansfield Road ⓣ 01865 271044 ⓦ www.club.ox.ac.uk ⓔ reception@club.ox.ac.uk ⓘ Disabled parking only

Burlington House £–££ A charming, friendly Victorian guesthouse, with tasteful modern décor and homely details. ⓐ 374 Banbury Road ⓣ 01865 513513 ⓕ 01865 311785 ⓦ www.burlington-house.co.uk ⓝ Bus: 2, 7, 25, 59, 93, 218, 700, S5 (stop: Hamilton Road) ⓘ Limited off-road parking

Holiday Inn Oxford £–££ This large, practical hotel on the outskirts of town offers affordable, family-friendly accommodation; a fully equipped gym, sauna and spa pool; and an indoor pool. ⓐ Peartree Roundabout, Woodstock Road ⓣ 0871 942 9086 ⓕ 01865 888333 ⓦ www.holidayinn.co.uk ⓝ Bus: 300 (stop: Pear Tree Park & Ride) ⓘ Free parking

Bath Place Hotel ££ Richard Burton and Elizabeth Taylor used to stay secretly at this quaint hotel, fashioned from a higgledy-piggledy group of 17th-century cottages hidden down a narrow cobbled alleyway. ⓐ 4–5 Bath Place ⓣ 01865 791812 ⓦ www.bathplace.co.uk ⓔ info@bathplace.co.uk

The Buttery Hotel ££ The only hotel on the prestigious Broad Street spans several interlinked townhouses and offers excellent value given its central location.  11–12 Broad Street  01865 811950  www.thebutteryhotel.co.uk

Ethos Hotel ££ A chic boutique hotel in a Victorian suburban townhouse, just south of the Thames, offering 'luxury with a conscience'. Expect smart, sumptuous rooms with super-king-sized beds and all mod cons, together with a variety of environmentally friendly features.  59 Western Road, Grandpont  01865 245800  www.ethoshotels.co.uk  info@ethoshotels.co.uk  Bus: 31, 34, 35, 44, X23 (stop: Whitehouse Road)

Mercure Oxford Eastgate Hotel ££ A modern hotel in a converted 17th-century coaching inn, with modest rooms and friendly service. Excellent value for its central location.  73 High Street  01865 248332  www.mercure.com  h668@accor.com  Limited pay parking

Apartments in Oxford ££–£££ A smart complex of luxury apartments near the railway station, ideal for overnight, short or long stays. Some apartments are specifically designed for wheelchair users.  58 St Thomas Street  01865 254000  01865 254001  www.oxstay.co.uk  Free parking

Malmaison ££–£££ This cutting-edge hotel offers the ultimate weekend 'escape' – inside the former city prison. The rooms are surprisingly sumptuous given that they were cells.  3 Oxford

Castle ☎ 01865 268400 🌐 www.malmaison-oxford.com
✉ oxford@malmaison.com ℗ Limited pay parking

Le Manoir aux Quat'Saisons £££ The ultimate in gourmet luxury.
The magnificent manor house hotel of the famous French chef
and Oxford *adopté* Raymond Blanc is set in beautiful gardens
13 km (8 miles) southeast of Oxford. 📍 Church Road, Great
Milton ☎ 01844 278881 🌐 www.manoir.com
✉ reservations@blanc.co.uk 🚆 Train to Oxford then taxi
℗ Free parking

Old Bank Hotel £££ A former Georgian bank has been handsomely
converted to create this fashionable, luxury hotel. The chic, buzzy
Quod brasserie serves unpretentious Mediterranean cuisine al
fresco from breakfast through to dinner. 📍 92–94 High Street
☎ 01865 799599 🌐 www.oldbank-hotel.co.uk
✉ reservations@oldbank-hotel.co.uk ℗ Limited pay parking

Old Parsonage Hotel £££ This beautiful 17th-century building
feels like a countryside retreat, despite its city-centre location.
📍 1 Banbury Road ☎ 01865 310210
🌐 www.oldparsonage-hotel.co.uk ✉ reception@oldparsonage-
hotel.co.uk 🚌 Bus: 2, 7, 14, 25, 59, 93, 218, S5 (stop: Bevington Road)

Randolph Hotel £££ The grand dame of Oxford, this five-star
hotel right in the heart of town offers the ultimate in comfort,
with its lavish rooms and luxurious spa. 📍 Beaumont Street
☎ 0844 879 9132 🌐 www.macdonaldhotels.co.uk/randolph
℗ Limited pay parking

THE BEST OF OXFORD

With over 900 buildings of architectural or historical interest within a square mile, there's plenty to see and do in Oxford.

TOP 10 ATTRACTIONS

- **Christ Church** Visit Oxford's largest college – the home of *Alice in Wonderland*, and a *Harry Potter* film set – with a cathedral in its grounds (see page 54).

- **University Church of St Mary the Virgin** A 127-step climb up the tower affords breathtaking views of the 'city of spires' (see page 47).

- **Bodleian Library** Tour Europe's first public library, and explore the vast network of underground passages and tunnels (see page 47).

- **Ashmolean Museum** Visit this world-famous collection of art and antiquities (see page 70).

- **Vaults & Garden Café** Linger over coffee or afternoon tea (see page 51), surrounded by some of Oxford's finest architecture, including the Radcliffe Camera.

- **Oxford University Museum of Natural History** Marvel at the dazzling display of zoological and geological treasures, complete with dodos and dinosaurs (see page 49).

- **Punting on the Thames** A once-in-a-lifetime experience. Do it in style, with a picnic and a bottle of champagne (see page 20).

- **Evensong** Experience choral music at an evensong service at Magdalen, Christ Church or New College (see pages 45, 54 and 45).

- **Magdalen College** Stroll in the gardens, deer park and along the riverside walk of this majestic college (see page 45).

- **Pitt Rivers Museum** A must-see museum, world renowned for its extraordinary array of ethnological artefacts and oddities (see page 49).

The Radcliffe Camera and All Souls College

Suggested itineraries

HALF-DAY: OXFORD IN A HURRY

If you have only a few hours, start at the top of St Mary's Church tower (on the High Street) for a view of the ancient Bodleian Library and colleges. From here, it is a stone's throw to the grandest college, Christ Church (via the Oriel Square entrance). Leave time for an idyllic stroll through Christ Church Meadow and along the riverbanks.

1 DAY: TIME TO SEE A LITTLE MORE

After the recommended half-day sightseeing, return to the High Street for lunch at Quod Brasserie, then add some shopping to your itinerary, in the choice boutiques of 'The High', or the quirky stores of the Covered Market. Alternatively, take in a museum. The world-famous Ashmolean Museum has exhibits to appeal to all the family; or visit the eccentric Pitt Rivers Museum and marvel at its whimsical but fascinating anthropological collections. End your day with a classical concert or dinner – there are some excellent restaurant choices in the Jericho district, including Loch Fyne and Brasserie Blanc.

2–3 DAYS: SHORT CITY-BREAK

Soak up college life (try to see Magdalen, New and Merton Colleges) and visit some more of the city's museums, including the impressive Natural History Museum. Don't miss a tour of the Bodleian, one of the oldest libraries in Europe, which each year adds a staggering 3 km (2 miles) of new materials to its shelves. And be sure to try your hand at punting … or a boat trip, at the very least!

LONGER: ENJOYING OXFORD TO THE FULL

A longer stay enables you to get under the skin of the city: go on a guided walk, discover Oxford's chequered past at Oxford Castle Unlocked, and peruse the multitude of plants at the Botanic Garden. In the evening, take in a chamber concert at the Sheldonian or the Holywell Room; or experience the eclectic mix of bars and restaurants along the Cowley Road. You may also have enough time to get out of town to visit Blenheim Palace, to tour the Thames or explore the Cotswold countryside.

Taking in the view from St Mary's Church tower is a must

Something for nothing

Oxford is a great destination for budget travellers, as there are plenty of sights and attractions to visit without the need to spend a single penny.

All the university museums are free, giving visitors unrivalled access to their world-class collections. Many colleges also offer free entry to visitors (most open afternoons only). In the city centre, these include All Souls, Corpus Christi, Exeter, Hertford, Jesus, Keble, Pembroke, St Edmund Hall, Worcester and Wolfson Colleges. It is also possible to peer through the porters' lodges into the elegant quadrangles of the other colleges, with their immaculately striped lawns and painstakingly tended gardens.

For free entertainment, you will find a whole host of street performers on the larger thoroughfares, ranging from morris dancers to fire-eaters. There is even a singing dog sometimes at the Carfax crossroads.

Oxford is blessed with more than its fair share of green spaces. Take time out from sightseeing to ramble across Port Meadow or hike the Thames Towpath. Or just while away your time on the riverbanks, watching the rowing 'eights' glide by.

When it rains

Don't despair if it rains during your stay! Oxford has plenty of attractions to cheer up the dullest, wettest day.

The city abounds in museums and galleries to suit all tastes and interests, from the ancient art treasures of the Ashmolean Museum to the complex scientific gadgets of the Museum of the History of Science. Keep kids amused by visiting the dungeons at Oxford Castle Unlocked; take them to the cinema; to Science Oxford Live, with its thrilling hands-on experiments; or go ice skating.

The open-top hop-on-hop-off City Sightseeing Bus is an ideal way of seeing the city or simply travelling from sight to sight in the rain, and there's always plenty of room on the lower floor.

If the rain persists, take refuge in the Covered Market with its tiny boutiques, cafés and restaurants. Indeed, the city is full of cosy cafés, bars and tea-shops, and there's always an excuse to nip in for a drink – whether it's for a quick mid-morning espresso pick-me-up, a luscious clotted-cream tea in the afternoon, or a pre-dinner cocktail with friends.

On arrival

There is no need to worry about your arrival in Oxford. Located in central England, just 80 km (50 miles) northwest of London, it is well served by road and rail networks. Once there, the city is small enough to navigate your way around on foot or by bicycle, and the Tourist Information Centre can provide detailed maps to help you.

FINDING YOUR FEET

Oxford is an extremely safe city with a low crime rate. Nonetheless, it is advisable to take commonsense precautions against petty crime (see page 92).

ORIENTATION

It is easy to find your way around Oxford as the city is so small. The **Tourist Information Centre** (ⓐ 15–16 Broad Street ⓦ www.visitoxford.org) has a range of maps for sale, and themed walking tours (see page 12) to help you get your bearings. The city has no central square, tourist focal point or main campus (as the university operates on a collegiate system), so most visitors orientate themselves around Carfax, a busy crossroads at the centre of the city, marked by the Carfax Tower (see page 66). Climb it for a bird's eye vista of the city centre to see Cornmarket Street to the north and Queen Street to the west – the city's two main shopping streets; the High Street (called 'The High') to the east, described by Nikolaus Pevsner as 'one of the world's great streets', with the bell tower of Magdalen College in the distance; and St Aldate's to the south, leading down past the distinctive octagonal Tom Tower of Christ Church to the River Thames (known in Oxford as the 'Isis').

Other equally impressive aerial viewpoints can be found up St Mary's Church tower (High Street, see page 47) or at the 11th-century **St Michael at the North Gate** (ⓐ Cornmarket Street ⓘ 01865 240940 ⓦ www.smng.org.uk ⓛ 10.30–17.00 daily Apr–Oct; 10.30–16.00 daily Nov–Mar), atop the tower of Oxford's oldest building.

◔ *Cycling is a convenient way of crossing the city*

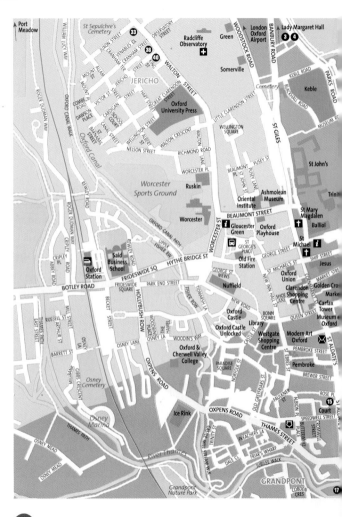

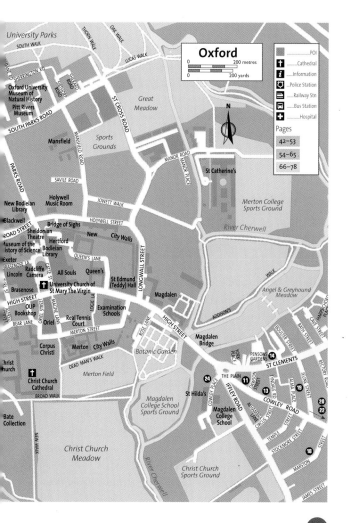

GETTING AROUND

The easiest way to explore the city centre is on foot, or to hire a bike and join the students as they hurtle over the cobbles. The **City Sightseeing Bus** is a convenient way to get around, if you are planning on visiting several attractions per day. It leaves every 20–30 minutes from various stops around the city, starting from Oxford railway station at 09.30 daily, and you can hop on and off at 19 stops (otherwise the round trip takes about 1 hour) at the main city sights (❶ 01865 790522 ⓦ www.citysightseeingoxford.com).

Most sights are within easy walking distance so, for the purposes of this book, bus stops are only included for sights more than a 5–10-minute walk from the city centre. Oxford has a comprehensive and frequent bus service with schedules posted at each stop (although most city centre stops serve outlying suburbs and villages). Hail the bus and pay the driver when you get on. Key routes include the 2 and 7, which head north up the Banbury Road; the 17 for Jericho; and the 1 and 5 for the Cowley Road.

To travel beyond the city centre, purchase a Dayrider ticket on any **Stagecoach Bus** (❶ 01865 772250 ⓦ www.stagecoachbus.com), for 24 hours of unlimited bus travel within the greater Oxford area; or consider a boat trip along the Thames (see page 20).

Taxis can be hailed in the street, picked up at ranks (at Gloucester Green, the train station and St Giles) or pre-booked by phone. Reliable companies include **ABC Taxis** (❶ 01865 770077), **City Taxis** (❶ 01865 201201) and **Radio Taxis** (❶ 01865 242424).

◆ *Punts on the Cherwell*

CAR HIRE

It is only worthwhile hiring a car if you are heading out of town to explore the surrounding countryside. There are several car hire companies including:

Avis (ⓐ 1 Abbey Road ⓣ 0844 544 6087 ⓦ www.avis.co.uk),
Thrifty (ⓐ Electric Avenue, Ferry Hinksey Road ⓣ 01865 250252 ⓦ www.thrifty.co.uk).

Check with your accommodation regarding parking arrangements as there are many restrictions within the city centre.

BIKE HIRE

There are more bicycles in Oxford than residents, and plenty of hire shops, including: **Bainton Bikes** (ⓐ 6 Bainton Road ⓣ 01865 365658 ⓦ www.baintonbikes.com ⓛ 08.00–21.30 Mon–Fri, 08.30–21.00 Sat & Sun), **Cycle King** (ⓐ 128–130 Cowley Road ⓣ 01865 728262 ⓦ www.cycleking.co.uk ⓛ 09.00–18.00 Mon–Sat, 10.00–17.00 Sun), **Walton Street Cycles** (ⓐ 78 Walton Street ⓣ 01865 311610 ⓦ www.spoke.co.uk ⓛ 08.45–17.45 Mon–Fri, 09.00–17.00 Sat, closed Sun).

If cycling sounds too much like hard work, tour in style with **Oxon Carts** (ⓣ 07747 024600 ⓦ www.oxoncarts.com), who offer a fast, fun, green way to get around town aboard smart rickshaws, with an Oxford undergraduate to answer all your questions as well as doing all the hard pedalling. They even offer guided pedal-powered city tours.

---

❿ *Oxford's compact city centre is easy to navigate*

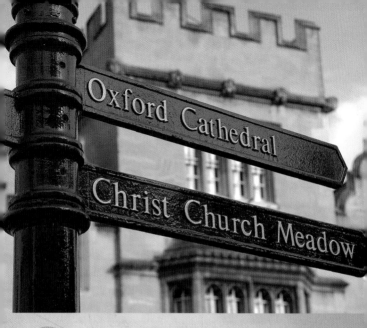

 THE CITY OF
Oxford

Introduction to Oxford city areas

For the purposes of this book, Oxford is split into three areas, divided by city-centre thoroughfares.

The first area, north of the magnificent High Street, is dominated by the honey-golden buildings of the colleges, packed round Broad Street, and the grandiose edifices of the Bodleian Library, the Sheldonian Theatre and the Radcliffe Camera. This area also contains major museums and some great pubs and river walks.

More historic colleges can be found south of 'The High'. Here is 'green' Oxford, with the Botanic Garden, and Christ Church Meadow at the confluence of the Rivers Isis and Cherwell. The Cowley Road presents a vibrant, urban side to Oxford, with its multi-ethnic restaurants and full-on student party vibe.

The third area, northwest of Queen and Cornmarket Streets, is more town than gown, and includes the quirky residential district of Jericho (centred on Walton Street), with its eclectic mix of trendy boutiques, bars and restaurants. It is also the main theatre district, and home to the Ashmolean Museum.

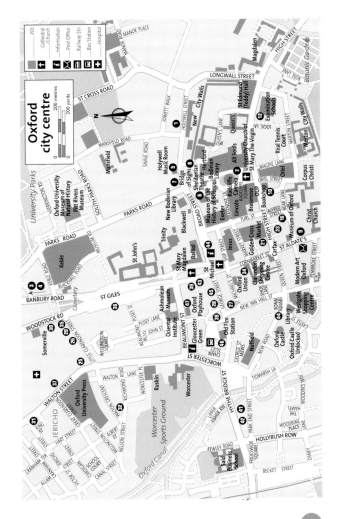

North of the High Street

This district represents the heart of Oxford and contains one of the finest architectural ensembles in Europe, centred on the Bodleian Library; some of the grandest colleges; and the university's main museums – all easily accessible on foot.

SIGHTS & ATTRACTIONS

Balliol College

Balliol is one of the oldest colleges, founded in 1263. For centuries, it was reserved for poor scholars and was considered the poor relation of the wealthier colleges, until it flourished in the Victorian era. Its list of alumni include authors Aldous Huxley and Graham Greene; former Prime Ministers Harold Macmillan and Edward Heath; and Mayor of London, Boris Johnson. ⓐ Broad Street ⓣ 01865 277777 ⓦ www.balliol.ox.ac.uk ⓛ 14.00–17.00/dusk daily ⓘ Admission charge

Brasenose College

Founded in 1509, the college takes its name from a bronze nose-shaped door knocker, the 'brazen nose', which now hangs in the dining hall. This 'nose' motif can be seen throughout the grounds, especially in the stonework surrounding the main gate. BNC prides itself on its excellent sporting reputation and counts comedian and TV presenter Michael Palin and Prime Minister David Cameron among former students. ⓐ Radcliffe Square ⓣ 01865 277830 ⓦ www.bnc.ox.ac.uk ⓛ 14.00–17.00 daily (summer); 14.00–16.30 daily (winter) ⓘ Admission charge

Bridge of Sighs

In narrow New College Lane you'll find both Hertford College's **'Bridge of Sighs'**, a 19th-century copy of the Venetian original, and the former home and rooftop observatory of 18th-century astronomer Edmund Halley. ➋ Holywell Street ☏ 01865 279555 ⓦ www.new.ox.ac.uk ⏱ 11.00–17.00 daily (Easter–early Oct); 14.00–16.00 daily (mid-Oct–Easter) ⓘ Admission charge (Easter–early Oct); free (mid-Oct–Easter)

⬥ *Hertford College's picturesque Bridge of Sighs*

Exeter College

The magnificent Victorian chapel of this 14th-century college contains a tapestry by textile designer (and Exeter graduate) William Morris. More recent alumni have included the actor Richard Burton; and writers Alan Bennett, Martin Amis, J R R Tolkien and Philip Pullman. ⓐ Turl Street ⓣ 01865 279600 ⓦ www.exeter.ox.ac.uk ⓛ 14.00–17.00 daily

Lady Margaret Hall

Beside the River Cherwell and named after Henry VII's mother, Lady Margaret Hall was the first college at Oxford to admit women – with just nine students – in 1878. Degrees for women

⬥ *James Gibbs' Radcliffe Camera, the earliest example of a circular library*

were not granted until 1920 (albeit 28 years before Cambridge
University). Exactly 100 years after its foundation, LMH started
accepting men, and now all undergraduate colleges are co-
educational and 48 per cent of all students at the university are
female. ⓐ Norham Gardens ☏ 01865 247300
ⓦ www.lmh.ox.ac.uk ⏰ Open by appointment only
ⓑ Bus: 2, 7, 14, 25, 59, 93, 218, S5 (stop: Bevington Road)

Magdalen College
Founded in 1458 by the Bishop of Winchester, Magdalen
(pronounced 'Maudlin') is considered one of the most beautiful
colleges in Oxford. With its own river walk, water meadow, deer
park (which is filled with rare fritillaries in April/May), cloisters,
three quadrangles and award-winning gardens, it also boasts
some of the most extensive grounds. The buildings are equally
impressive, most notably the 15th-century cloisters, bell tower
and chapel – home to the celebrated chapel choir, which can be
heard during term time at evensong (⏰ 18.00 Wed–Mon).
ⓐ High Street ☏ 01865 276000 📠 01865 276030
ⓦ www.magd.ox.ac.uk ⏰ 12.00–18.00 daily (July–Sept); 13.00–
18.00/dusk daily (Oct–June) ⓘ Admission charge

New College
Hardly 'new', this college was founded as early as 1379. It was,
however, the first to be constructed around a quadrangle plan.
The idyllic gardens contain a section of the city's original 12th-
century wall, giving the college a castle-like appearance. The
chapel is noted for its painted glass windows by Sir Joshua
Reynolds, its disturbing statue of the risen Lazarus by Epstein,

and its internationally renowned chapel choir. College luminaries include authors Virginia Woolf and John Fowles; and actor Hugh Grant. ⓐ Holywell Street ⓣ 01865 279 555 ⓕ 01865 279 590 ⓦ www.new.ox.ac.uk ⓛ 11.00–17.00 Easter–early Oct, 14.00–16.00 rest of year ⓘ Admission charge (Easter–Oct); free (Nov–Easter)

Radcliffe Camera

The domed 'Rad Cam' is one of Oxford's most iconic buildings and England's first circular library. Designed by James Gibbs with funding from John Radcliffe, it was completed in 1749. It now serves as a reading room for the Bodleian Library. ⓐ Radcliffe Square ⓣ 01865 277162 ⓦ www.bodley.ox.ac.uk ⓔ reader.services@bodleian.ox.ac.uk ⓘ Access through Bodleian Library guided tours only (see page 47)

St Edmund Hall

'Teddy Hall' is considered Oxford's oldest surviving educational establishment. Founded in the early 12th century, it only became a full university college in 1957. The chapel contains some striking stained glass by Pre-Raphaelite artists William Morris and Edward Burne-Jones. The Norman church within the college grounds now houses the college library. ⓐ Queen's Lane ⓣ 01865 279000 ⓕ 01865 279090 ⓦ www.seh.ox.ac.uk ⓛ 12.00–16.00 Mon–Fri, closed Sat & Sun (in term time)

Sheldonian Theatre

The Sheldonian was designed and constructed in the style of a Roman theatre by the young Christopher Wren between

1664 and 1668 while he was Professor of Astronomy at the University. A major concert venue, it is also used for degree ceremonies and the annual Encaenia, at which honorary degrees are conferred on distinguished people. The interior is made entirely of wood, and the eight-sided cupola boasts superb city vistas. ⓐ Broad Street ❶ 01865 277299 ⓦ www.sheldon.ox.ac.uk 🕓 10.00–12.30 & 14.00–16.30 Mon–Sat, closed Sun (Mar–Oct); 10.00–12.30 & 14.00–15.30 Mon–Sat, closed Sun (Nov–Feb) ❶ Ring before visiting, as theatre is regularly closed for concerts

University Church of St Mary the Virgin

The largest of Oxford's parish churches is best known for its university sermon (most Sundays during term time) and the views from the top of its fine 13th-century tower. ⓐ High Street ❶ 01865 279111 ⓦ www.university-church.ox.ac.uk ⓔ university.church@ox.ac.uk 🕓 09.00–18.00 daily (July & Aug); 09.00–17.00 daily (Sept–June) ❶ Admission charge (tower only)

CULTURE

Bodleian Library

Of Oxford's 200-plus libraries, none is as celebrated as the Bodleian, founded in 1602 as Europe's first public library by Sir Thomas Bodley, a Fellow of Merton College. With over eight million books and manuscripts, including one copy of every new book published in the UK, it ranks among the world's greatest libraries. Visits are by guided tour only, and include the **Radcliffe Camera**; the 17th-century **Convocation House**, where the university's governing body meets; **Duke Humfrey's Medieval Library**, the oldest of the nine reading rooms in 'the Bod', which doubled as the Hogwarts Library in the *Harry Potter* movies; and the **Divinity School** – a masterpiece of English Gothic architecture with its impressive fan-vaulted ceiling.

ⓐ Broad Street ⓣ 01865 277178 ⓦ www.bodleian.ox.ac.uk ⓔ tours@bodleian.ox.ac.uk ⓛ 09.00–17.00 Mon–Fri, 09.00–16.30 Sat, 11.00–17.00 Sun. Tours: 10.30, 11.30, 14.00 & 15.00 Mon–Sat, 11.30, 14.00 & 15.00 Sun; short tours (30 mins): 16.00 daily; extended tours (90 mins): 10.00 Sat, 11.15 Sun ⓘ Admission charge

Museum of the History of Science

This quirky museum contains an impressive selection of around 15,000 scientific instruments and curious gadgets. It is

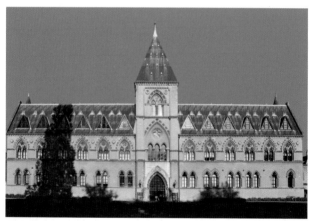

◔ *Shadows falling on the Natural History Museum*

housed in the world's oldest surviving purpose-built museum building (once home to the treasures of the Ashmolean Museum). Of particular note are the collections of astrolabes and sundials, Einstein's blackboard, the Marconi Collection of radio equipment, and author Lewis Carroll's photographic kit.

ⓐ Broad Street ☎ 01865 277280 ⓦ www.mhs.ox.ac.uk
🕐 12.00–17.00 Tues–Fri, 10.00–17.00 Sat, 14.00–17.00 Sun, closed Mon

Oxford University Museum of Natural History

Described as a 'cathedral to science' and bathed in light from its high-glass ceiling, the museum's lofty Victorian-Gothic building alone is worth a visit. Add gigantic dinosaur skeletons, fossils and space rocks; the last remains of the Oxford Dodo; a multitude of animal and insect specimens; countless hands-on activities and you have a fascinating and educational museum that appeals to all members of the family.

ⓐ Parks Road ☎ 01865 272950 ⓦ www.oum.ox.ac.uk
🕐 10.00–17.00 daily Ⓝ Bus: 6, 18, 52, 206, 853, S2, S3 (stop: Radcliffe Infirmary)

Pitt Rivers Museum

With its dim lighting and veritable treasure trove of anthropological objects, an old-fashioned air pervades this world-famous museum, founded in 1884 with a gift of around 18,000 items from Lieutenant General Augustus Henry Lane Fox Pitt Rivers. Borrow a torch at the entrance to rummage in the display drawers and to browse the rows of glass cabinets, each crammed full of bizarre yet fascinating ethnographic artefacts from tools and textiles to masks and magic charms. South Parks Road (entry via the Oxford University Museum of Natural History) 01865 270927 www.prm.ox.ac.uk 10.00–16.30 Tues–Sun, 12.00–16.30 Mon Bus: 6, 18, 52, 206, 853, S2, S3 (stop: Radcliffe Infirmary)

RETAIL THERAPY

Blackwell Oxford's oldest and most celebrated bookseller boasts several shops in Broad Street. 48–51 Broad Street 01865 792792 http://bookshop.blackwell.co.uk oxford@blackwell.co.uk 09.00–18.30 Mon–Sat, 11.00–17.00 Sun

Ducker & Son A pair of traditional hand-sewn shoes from this old-fashioned bespoke shoemaker will last a lifetime. 6 Turl Street 01865 242461 www.duckerandson.co.uk sales@duckerandson.co.uk 09.00–17.30 Mon–Fri, 10.00–17.30 Sat, closed Sun

Oxford Cheese Company This tiny store within the Covered Market offers over 250 farmhouse cheeses, including the tangy Oxford Isis and the creamy, award-winning Oxford Blue. Avenue 1, 17 Covered Market 01865 721420 www.oxfordfinefood.com sales@oxfordfinefood.com 08.00–17.30 Mon–Sat, closed Sun

The Varsity Shop The leading supplier of Oxford University College clothing stocks a huge assortment of garments and accessories from rugby shirts to scarves and cufflinks for students and visitors. ➋ 13 Broad Street ➊ 01865 244000 ⓦ www.varsityshop.co.uk ⓔ shop@varsityshop.co.uk ⓛ 09.00–17.30 Mon–Fri, 10.00–17.00 Sat, closed Sun

TAKING A BREAK

Edamamé £ ❶ A tiny, popular restaurant serving authentic, affordable Japanese home cooking, with sushi nights every Thursday. ➋ 15 Holywell Street ➊ 01865 246916 (no reservations) ⓦ www.edamame.co.uk ⓛ 11.30–14.30 Wed, 11.30–14.30 & 17.00–20.30 Thur–Sat, 12.00–15.30 Sun, closed Mon & Tues

Vaults & Garden Café £ ❷ This atmospheric café in the vaulted basement of St Mary's Church serves locally sourced, seasonal organic lunches and teas, but its real appeal is the sunny herb-scented garden. ➋ University Church of St Mary the Virgin, Radcliffe Square ➊ 01865 279112 ⓦ www.vaultsandgarden.com ⓛ 10.00–17.00 Mon–Fri, 08.30–17.00 Sat & Sun

Cherwell Boathouse ££ ❸ A small, country-style restaurant and café, offering top-notch modern British food and fine wines on the riverbank beside the punt station. ➋ 50 Bardwell Road ➊ 01865 552746 ⓦ www.cherwellboathouse.co.uk ⓛ 12.00–14.15 (last orders) & 18.00–21.30 (last orders) daily ⓝ Bus: 2, 7, 14, 25, 59, 94, 218, S5 (stop: Park Town)

Gee's ££ ❹ It is hard to beat Gee's restaurant for a romantic dinner. Housed in a beautiful Victorian glass conservatory, there

is low-key jazz on Sunday nights. ⓐ 61 Banbury Road
ⓣ 01865 553540 ⓦ www.gees-restaurant.co.uk ⓛ 12.00–14.30 &
18.00–22.00 Mon–Thur, 12.00–14.30 & 18.00–22.30 Fri & Sat,
12.00–15.30 & 18.00–22.00 Sun ⓝ Bus: 2, 7, 14, 25, 59, 93, 218, S5
(stop: Bevington Road)

AFTER DARK

Performance arts
Holywell Music Room ❺ Haydn once performed here in
Europe's first purpose-built concert hall, and it has remained a
popular, intimate venue for recitals and chamber concerts,
including Coffee Concerts most Sundays at 11.15. ⓐ Holywell
Street ⓣ 01865 305305 ⓦ www.music.ox.ac.uk/facilities/
Holywell-music-room.html; www.coffeeconcerts.com

⬭ *Stop for a pint in The Kings Arms*

Sheldonian Theatre ❻ In 1733 Handel was presented with a doctor's degree in music here and it has been a popular concert venue ever since, for international performers and the Oxford Philomusica Orchestra. ⓐ Broad Street ❶ 01865 277299; Music at Oxford: 01865 242865 ⓦ www.sheldon.ox.ac.uk; www.musicatoxford.com; www.oxfordphil.com

Pubs

Kings Arms ❼ This former coaching inn is a popular student pub – especially lively in June when they spill onto the pavement in post-exam revelry. ⓐ 40 Holywell Street ❶ 01865 242369 ⓦ www.kingsarmsoxford.co.uk ⓔ KingsArmsOxford@youngs.co.uk ❶ 10.30–00.00 daily

The Turf Tavern ❽ A snug, pint-sized 13th-century alehouse nestled down an alleyway with a superb choice of draught beers, real ales and ciders; and a courtyard garden with braziers for toasting marshmallows in winter. ⓐ 4–5 Bath Place (off Holywell Street) ❶ 01865 243235 ⓦ www.theturftavern.co.uk ❶ 11.00–23.00 Mon–Sat, 11.00–22.30 Sun

South of the High Street

This district contains some of Oxford's most prestigious colleges and embraces green oases and river walks, as well as the colourful, non-conformist Cowley Road (easily reachable by bus from the High Street) with its many bars, clubs, restaurants and multi-ethnic shops.

SIGHTS & ATTRACTIONS

Botanic Garden

Britain's oldest botanic garden was created in 1621 on the site of an old Jewish burial ground. It is a haven from the bustle of the city centre, and contains one of the most diverse plant collections in the world. ❸ Rose Lane/High Street ❶ 01865 286690 Ⓦ www.botanic-garden.ox.ac.uk ⏰ 09.00–16.30 daily (Nov–Feb); 09.00–17.00 daily (Mar, Apr, Sept & Oct); 09.00–18.00 daily (May–Aug) ❶ Admission charge: daily (Mar–Oct); Sat & Sun (Nov–Feb)

Christ Church

If you have time for only one college, visit Oxford's largest – Christ Church – founded by Henry VIII in 1546, with its celebrated chapel and world-renowned choir; its landmark tower – the Tom Tower – built by Sir Christopher Wren; and its internationally important collection of Old Master paintings. No fewer than 13 British prime ministers were educated here; its most celebrated graduate was perhaps the maths don Charles Dodgson (aka Lewis Carroll), who wrote his legendary Alice

stories for Alice Liddell, daughter of the dean. More recently, the
Tudor dining hall was a film set for Hogwarts in J K Rowling's
Harry Potter stories. ❷ St Aldate's ❶ 01865 286573;
Picture Gallery: 01865 276172 🕨 www.chch.ox.ac.uk
❸ tourism@chch.ox.ac.uk 🕓 09.00–17.00 Mon–Sat, 14.00–17.00
Sun. Picture Gallery: 10.30–17.00 Mon–Sat, 14.00–17.00 Sun
(May–Sept); 10.30–13.00 & 14.00–16.30 Mon–Sat, 14.00–16.30
Sun (Oct–Apr) ❶ Admission charge

Corpus Christi College

Corpus Christi was founded in 1517 by Richard Fox, Bishop of
Winchester. The college boasts 117 gargoyles, but its best-loved

🔺 *Britain's oldest botanic garden*

feature is the unusual golden pelican sundial in the beautiful quad. It operates by both sun and moon and is set to Old Oxford time – 5 minutes behind GMT. ⓐ Merton Street ❶ 01865 276700 ⓦ www.ccc.ox.ac.uk ⏰ 13.30–16.30 daily

Examination Schools

This imposing Victorian building was built for university lectures and, in late May and early June, degree examinations. All students are required to wear a gown, mortar board or cap and sub-fusc (formal black and white clothing). They often also wear a carnation in their buttonhole – white for the first examination, pink thereafter and red for the final one. ⓐ 75–81 High Street ⓦ www.admin.ox.ac.uk/schools ⏰ Closed to the public

Merton College

Merton boasts the oldest quadrangle – Mob Quad – completed in 1378 and the blueprint for most quads in Oxford and Cambridge. It also houses the world's oldest academic library, with a first edition of *The Canterbury Tales*, Chaucer's astrolabe and the first Bible printed in Welsh. Famous alumni include the poet T S Eliot and J R R Tolkien, author of *The Hobbit* and *The Lord of the Rings*.

Across the road, the **Real Tennis Court** (a forerunner of lawn tennis, popular in the 16th century) can be visited for a small fee. The **Dead Man's Walk** runs alongside Merton Field to the Botanic Garden. It is allegedly the path taken by Oxford's Jewish community centuries ago to carry their dead from the synagogue to the Jewish burial ground (now the Botanic

△ *Merton College seen across Merton Field*

Garden), as they were not permitted to pass through the city centre. ⓐ Merton Street ❶ 01865 276310 ⓦ www.merton.ox.ac.uk ❷ 14.00–16.00 Mon–Fri, 10.00–16.00 Sat & Sun ❶ Admission charge

CULTURE

Bate Collection of Musical Instruments

The Bate Collection, housed in the Faculty of Music, is one of the world's finest collections of musical instruments, ranging from the alphorn to the Javanese gamelan. The historical harpsichords are kept in playing condition and used in occasional concerts here. ⓐ Faculty of Music, St Aldate's ❶ 01865 276139 ❶ 01865 286261 ⓦ www.bate.ox.ac.uk ❷ 14.00–17.00 Mon–Fri, 10.00–12.00 Sat (during term time), closed Sun

Modern Art Oxford

Hidden down a backstreet in an old brewery warehouse, the MAO hosts highly acclaimed exhibitions of international contemporary art, together with a programme of workshops and entertainment. ⓐ 30 Pembroke Street ❶ 01865 722733 ⓦ www.modernartoxford.org.uk ❷ 10.00–17.00 Tues & Wed, 10.00–22.00 Thur–Sat, 12.00–17.00 Sun, closed Mon

Museum of Oxford

The only museum dedicated to the colourful history of the city. A maze of rooms on two floors portrays prehistoric times to the present; literary connections; the Civil War (when Charles I made

🔺 *Alice's Shop is packed with* Alice in Wonderland *merchandise*

Oxford his base); and the growth of river trade, industry and the university. ⓐ Town Hall, St Aldate's ⓣ 01865 252761 ⓦ www.museumofoxford.org.uk ⓔ museum@oxford.gov.uk ⓛ 10.00–17.00 Tues–Fri (last admission 16.30), 12.00–17.00 Sat & Sun (last admission 16.30), closed Mon

RETAIL THERAPY

Alice's Shop This tiny ancient curiosity shop is a must-see for fans of Lewis Carroll's *Through the Looking Glass*. Here the real-life Alice Liddell used to buy her sweets in the 1830s. Today it is crammed full of *Alice* memorabilia. ⓐ 83 St Aldate's ⓣ 01865 723793 ⓦ www.aliceinwonderlandshop.co.uk ⓔ info@aliceinwonderlandshop.co.uk ⓛ 09.30–19.00 daily (July & Aug); 10.30–17.00 daily (Sept–June)

Antiques on High An Aladdin's cave of treasures, run by over 30 dealers, awaits the keen browser at Oxford's favourite venue for buying antiques. ⓐ 85 High Street ⓣ 01865 251075 ⓦ www.antiquesonhigh.co.uk ⓔ enquiries@antiquesonhigh.co.uk ⓛ 10.00–17.00 Mon–Sat, 11.00–17.00 Sun

The OUP Bookshop Books have been published in Oxford for more than 500 years. During the 19th century, the Oxford University Press was the city's largest employer, and this shop has been its shop window since 1872. ⓐ 116–117 High Street ⓣ 01865 242913 ⓦ www.oup.com ⓛ 09.30–18.00 Mon–Sat, 11.00–17.00 Sun

TAKING A BREAK

G&D's £ ❾ Expect to queue at this traditional-style ice-cream parlour with its fun flavours, including Oxford Blue (with blueberries), mint Aero and smelly bee (lavender and honey).
ⓐ 94 St Aldate's ⓣ 01865 245952 ⓦ www.gdcafe.com
ⓛ 08.00–00.00 daily

The Mission Mexican Grill £ ❿ The authentic burritos (to eat in or take away) at this popular Mexican fast-food joint make a speedy, filling lunch for shoppers and sightseers, washed down with a refreshing Mexican beer. ⓐ King Edward Street
ⓣ 01865 722020 ⓦ www.missionburritos.co.uk
ⓔ info@missionburritos.co.uk ⓛ 11.00–22.00 Sun–Wed, 11.00–23.00 Thur–Sat

Café CoCo £–££ ⓫ A laid-back, colonial-style brasserie serving sensational brunches (till noon), affordable cocktails and posh pizzas. ⓐ 23 Cowley Road ⓣ 01865 200232
ⓦ www.cafe-coco.co.uk ⓛ 10.00–23.00 Sun–Wed, 10.00–00.00 Thur, 10.00–00.30 Fri & Sat ⓝ Bus: 1, 5, 10, 12, 48, 49, 101, 103, 104, U5 (stop: The Plain)

Grand Café £–££ ⓬ This historic, listed building was the site of the first coffee house in England in the mid-17th century. With its plush interior of mirrors, marble pillars and palms, it remains *the* place for coffee and cake or a fancy high tea. ⓐ 84 High Street ⓣ 01865 204463 ⓦ www.thegrandcafe.co.uk ⓛ 09.00–18.00 & 19.00–23.00 Mon–Sat, 09.00–18.00 Sun

Kazbar £–££ ⑬ A sophisticated crowd flock here for high-quality tapas and sangría in a sumptuous and exotic, lantern-lit Moroccan ambience. ⓐ 25–27 Cowley Road ① 01865 202920 ⓦ www.kazbar.co.uk ① 16.00–00.00 Mon–Thur, 16.00–00.30 Fri, 12.00–00.30 Sat, 12.00–00.00 Sun ⓝ Bus: 1, 5, 10, 12, 48, 49, 101, 103, 104, U5 (stop: The Plain)

Fisher's ££ ⑭ This informal, sea-themed bistro serves the best fish and seafood in Oxford – everything from humble fish and chips to extravagant shellfish platters. ⓐ 36–37 St Clements ① 01865 243003 ⓕ 01865 243003 ⓦ www.fishers-restaurant.com ① 12.00–14.30 & 18.00–22.30 Mon–Sat, 12.30–15.00 & 18.00–22.00 Sun ⓝ Bus: 7C, 8, 9, 13, 15, 108, 118, 275, 280, U1, X13, X23 (stop: St Clements)

△ *Have afternoon tea in England's oldest coffee house, the Grand Café*

Shanghai 30's ££ ⑮ Old-fashioned jazz, Chinese antiques and attentive service conjure up the exuberant atmosphere of 1930s Shanghai (the 'Paris of the Orient') in this upmarket Chinese restaurant. ⓐ 82 St Aldate's ⓣ 01865 242230 ⓦ www.shanghai30s.com ⓔ contact@shanghai30s.com ⓛ 18.00–23.00 Mon, 12.00–14.30 & 18.00–23.00 Tues–Fri, 12.00–23.00 Sat, 12.00–22.30 Sun

AFTER DARK

Bars & pubs
Bear Inn ⑯ Oxford's oldest pub (dating back to 1242) is a favourite with both town and gown, famed for its collection of ties, donated by customers over the years in exchange for a pint. ⓐ 6 Alfred Street ⓣ 01865 728164 ⓦ www.fullers.co.uk ⓔ bearinn@fullers.co.uk ⓛ 11.00–23.00 Mon–Sat, 11.00–22.30 Sun

Head of the River ⑰ This spacious pub, with its sunny terrace beside the Cherwell River, is a popular haunt for students, tourists and locals, especially after a lazy afternoon of punting, or to celebrate a boat race win. ⓐ Folly Bridge ⓣ 01865 721600 ⓦ www.fullershotels.com ⓔ headoftheriver@fullers.co.uk ⓛ 11.30–23.00 daily

The Oxford Blue ⑱ A smart, friendly locals' bar, serving real ale near the university Rugby Club and the playing fields, where on 6 May 1954 Roger Bannister, an Oxford medical student, set the new world mile record of 3 minutes 59.4 seconds – the first mile ever run in under 4 minutes. ⓐ 32 Marston Street

☎ 01865 723898 ⓦ www.theoxfordblue.com
ⓔ info@theoxfordblue.com ⓛ 17.00–23.00 Sun–Thur, 12.00–
00.00 Fri & Sat ⓝ Bus: 1, 5, 10, 12, 48, 49, 101, 103, 104, U5 (stop:
James Street)

Cinema

Ultimate Picture Palace ⓲ This single-screen independent
cinema shows classic old movies, cult films and independent
international titles. ⓐ Jeune Street (off Cowley Road)
☎ 01865 245288 ⓦ www.ultimatepicturepalace.com
ⓔ info@ultimatepicturepalace.com ⓝ Bus: 1, 5, 10, 12, 48, 49, 101,
103, 104, U5 (stop: James Street)

Clubs & live acts

The Backroom at the Bully ⓴ A simple spit-and-sawdust
backroom at the Bullingdon Arms pub is a popular clubbing
venue, with theme nights ranging from trance to blues.
ⓐ 162 Cowley Road ☎ 01865 244516 ⓛ 12.00–00.00 Mon, Wed &
Thur, 12.00–02.00 Tues, Fri & Sat, 12.00–23.30 Sun ⓝ Bus: 1, 5, 10,
12, 48, 49, 101, 103, 104, U5 (stop: James Street)

Escape ㉑ An intimate bar and club complex above the covered
market, with two dance floors playing music from R'n'B and
Latino to ethnic and dance. ⓐ 9A High Street ☎ 01865 246766
☎ 01865 728609 ⓦ http://escapeoxford.com ⓛ Mon–Sat 17.00–
04.00, closed Sun

O2 Academy ㉒ Oxford's premier live music venue regularly
draws top indie bands and international big name bands, often

prior to their major tours. It is also one of the town's busiest nightclubs, attracting a young, flirty crowd. ⓐ 190 Cowley Road ⓣ 01865 813500; box office: 0844 477 2000 ⓦ www.o2academyoxford.co.uk ⓛ 18.30–04.00 daily; box office: 12.00–16.00 Mon–Sat, closed Sun ⓝ Bus: 1, 5, 10, 12, 48, 49, 101, 103, 104, U5 (stop: Manzil Way)

The Spin ㉓ Rated as one of the finest jazz clubs in Britain, with superb acoustics and an intimate candlelit atmosphere, drawing top jazz musicians from the UK and beyond. ⓐ 129 High Street (above the Wheatsheaf Pub) ⓣ 01865 721156 ⓦ www.spinjazz.com ⓛ Gigs on Thur during term time: doors open 20.15; bands play 21.00–11.00

Performance arts
Jacqueline du Pré Music Building ㉔ The 'JdP' at St Hilda's College is a living memorial to the former student and a popular venue for international chamber music concerts, and for recitals by young, up-and-coming soloists. ⓐ Cowley Place ⓣ 01865 276821 ⓦ www.st-hildas.ox.ac.uk ⓝ Bus: 1, 5, 10, 12, 48, 49, 101, 103, 104, U5 (stop: The Plain)

Northwest city centre

Bounded by Queen Street to the south with Cornmarket and St
Giles Streets to the east, this district stretches northwards
beyond the Ashmolean Museum, to embrace the bohemian
district of Jericho with its trendy boutiques, bars and
restaurants. Central sights are easily accessible on foot, and bus
17 runs through the heart of Jericho.

SIGHTS & ATTRACTIONS

Carfax Tower

This 23-m (75-ft) tower is all that remains of the medieval
church of St Martin, destroyed in the 18th century to widen the
roads at the junction of St Aldate's, Queen Street, Cornmarket
Street and The High – hence the name, from the French
carrefour ('crossroads'). Climb the tightly winding 99 steps for
impressive aerial views (come early to avoid crowds), or admire
the two mechanical 'quarter boys', who chime bells every
quarter-hour on the eastern façade. ⓐ Queen Street
ⓘ 01865 792653 ⓦ www.citysightseeingoxford.com
ⓛ 10.00–15.30 daily (Nov–Feb); 10.00–16.30 daily (Mar & Oct);
10.00–17.30 daily (Apr–Sept) ⓘ Admission charge

Nuffield College

With its eye-catching green conical spire, this was the first
Oxford college to have a subject specialisation (Social Sciences)
and the first to be graduate-only. It takes its name from William
Morris (later Lord Nuffield), who single-handedly changed the

🔺 *The view down the High Street from the Carfax Tower*

face of the city. As a boy, Morris started making bicycles in 1901 at 48 High Street, progressing on to motorcycles until, by 1912, he produced his first car – the 'bull-nosed Morris' (so-named for its bullet-shaped radiator). It was so successful that he opened a car assembly plant at Cowley, east of Oxford. Sales rose from just 204 in 1918 to over 55,000 in 1925, by which time Morris Motors Ltd was producing 41 per cent of all British cars. His success attracted related industries and by 1936 Oxford had become one of the country's most prosperous cities. In 1937 William Morris provided the funds to build Nuffield College. His company is best remembered for its production of MG and

⏏ *St George's Tower, Oxford Castle*

Morris Minor cars. The Cowley plant, now owned by BMW and producing Minis, remains the largest industrial employer in Oxfordshire. ⓐ New Road ⓣ 01865 278500 ⓕ 01865 278621 ⓦ www.nuffield.ox.ac.uk ⓛ 09.00–17.00 daily

Oxford Castle and Oxford Castle Unlocked

Oxford Castle was built for William the Conqueror in 1071. During the Civil War, having fled London, Charles I used it as his main residence, but it was destroyed by Parliamentary troops, although the prison remained. Tour the castle to discover its chequered history, to admire views atop St George's Tower and to visit the dungeons. ⓐ 44–46 New Road ⓣ 01865 260666 ⓦ www.oxfordcastleunlocked.co.uk ⓔ info@oxfordcastleunlocked.co.uk ⓛ 10.00–17.30 daily (last tour 16.10) ⓘ Admission charge

Oxford Union

The Oxford Union is the university's oldest, largest student club and the world's most prestigious debating society. Founded in 1823 as a forum for the debate and discussion of controversial issues, many of its members have gone on to become prominent figures in the world of politics, including William Gladstone, Edward Heath, Benazir Bhutto, Tony Blair and David Cameron. ⓐ Frewin Court ⓣ 01865 241353 ⓦ www.oxford-union.org ⓛ Closed to the public

Port Meadow

Mentioned as common land in the Domesday Book, to this day Freemen of Oxford and Commoners of Wolvercote exercise grazing rights on this pastureland between river and railway. Known for its profusion of wild flowers and birdlife it is a lovely, hour-long stroll up the western flank of the meadow, via **The Perch** (a riverside pub, www.the-perch.co.uk) for refreshment, to the celebrated **Trout Inn** (www.thetroutoxford.co.uk) at Wolvercote – a favourite watering-hole of Lewis Carroll, C S Lewis and, more recently, TV's Inspector Morse. Access via Walton Well Road, Aristotle Lane or Wolvercote Bus: 17 (stop: School)

Worcester College

Worcester is slightly off the beaten track, but you will be richly rewarded by its 10.5 hectares (26 acres) of magnificent grounds, ablaze with flowers and pleasant shady lakeside walks.
Worcester Street 01865 278300 01865 278369
www.worc.ox.ac.uk 14.00–17.00 daily

CULTURE

Ashmolean Museum

The world's oldest public museum of art and antiquities opened in 1683, created to house local lawyer Elias Ashmole's gift of the Tradescant collection – an eccentric collection displayed in the basement, including Guy Fawkes' lantern. Following a £61-million redevelopment in 2009, a magnificent new building holds this world-acclaimed treasure trove. Beaumont Street
01865 278000 www.ashmolean.org 10.00–18.00 Tues–Sun & Bank Holiday Mon, closed Mon; restaurant: 10.00–22.00 Tues–Sat, 10.00–18.00 Sun, closed Mon

RETAIL THERAPY

Oxford's two main thoroughfares here – Cornmarket and Queen Streets – contain countless high-street chains, while Jericho has a handful of smaller, more individual boutiques.

Central Furniture A trendy store focusing on cutting-edge furniture, innovative kitchenware and funky gadgets for the office or home. ⓐ 33–35 Little Clarendon Street ⓣ 01865 311141 ⓦ www.central-furniture.co.uk ⓛ 09.30–18.00 Mon–Sat, 11.30–17.30 Sun ⓝ Bus: 6, 18, 52, 206, 853, S2, S3 (stop: Radcliffe Infirmary)

Maison Blanc Raymond Blanc's bakery-patisserie serves baked bread, takeaway sandwiches, handmade chocolates and mouth-watering cakes, and there's a tearoom at the back. ⓐ 3 Woodstock Road ⓣ 01865 510974 ⓦ www.maisonblanc.co.uk ⓛ 07.30–19.00 Mon–Sat, 08.30–17.00 Sun ⓝ Bus: 6, 18, 52, 206, 853, S2, S3 (stop: Radcliffe Infirmary)

The Town Garden This tiny shop brings the countryside into town with its gorgeous collection of plant pots, books, produce, chunky tools and gift ideas for garden lovers. ⓐ 1 North Parade Avenue ⓣ 01865 552626 ⓦ www.thetowngarden.com ⓔ sales@thetowngarden.com ⓛ 09.30–17.00 Mon–Sat, closed Sun ⓝ Bus: 2, 7, 14, 25, 59, 93, 218, S5 (stop: Bevington Road)

🔺 *Visit Raymond Blanc's famous* pâtisserie *and indulge in some delicious treats*

TAKING A BREAK

The Big Bang £ ㉕ *Restaurant* magazine voted this restaurant 'the finest sausage and mash in Britain, with hearty helpings of bangers and mash, and all ingredients sourced from within a 20-mile radius'. The Tuesday evening jazz club in the cellar is the best in town. ❸ 124 Walton Street ❶ 01865 511441 ⓦ www.thebigbangoxford.co.uk ❷ 08.00–15.00 & 17.00–23.00 Mon–Fri, 09.00–23.00 Sat, 09.00–21.00 Sun ⓝ Bus: 17 (stop: Walton Street)

Al-Andalus £–££ ㉖ A cosy, informal tapas bar with an authentic Spanish feel, enhanced on Friday and Saturday nights by live Spanish dancing. Try the paella or some tapas (great for vegetarians), washed down by a jug of sangría. ❸ 10 Little Clarendon Street ❶ 01865 516688 ⓦ www.tapasoxford.co.uk ❷ 12.00–15.00 & 17.00–late Mon–Thur, 12.00–late Fri–Sun ⓝ Bus: 6, 18, 52, 206, 853, S2, S3 (stop: Radcliffe Infirmary)

Chutney's £–££ ㉗ A hugely popular Indian restaurant, serving refined southern Indian cuisine in a relaxed, café-style setting. ❸ 36 St Michael's Street ❶ 01865 724241 ⓦ www.chutneysoxford.com ❷ 12.00–14.00 & 18.00–23.30 daily

Jamie's £–££ ㉘ This simple rustic Italian-style restaurant (owned by TV celebrity chef Jamie Oliver) draws a trendy crowd with its alluring seasonal menu. Try an antipasti platter, followed by 'lamb chop lollipops' with 'funky chips'. The all-

Italian wines are served by the glass, bottle or pichet.
ⓐ 24–26 George Street ☎ 01865 838383
ⓦ www.jamieoliver.com/italian
ⓔ oxford.admin@jamiesitalian.com ⏱ 12.00–23.00 daily

Pierre Victoire £–££ ㉔ A tiny, candlelit bistro serving such
authentic French dishes as cassoulet, bouillabaisse, *moules frites*
and *fondue savoyarde*. ⓐ 9 Little Clarendon Street
☎ 01865 316616 ⓦ www.pierrevictoire.co.uk ⏱ 12.00–14.30 &
18.00–23.00 Mon–Sat, 12.00–15.30 & 18.00–22.00 Sun ⓝ Bus: 6,
18, 52, 206, 853, S2, S3 (stop: Radcliffe Infirmary)

Browns ££ ㉚ This big, bustling restaurant with its large palms
and colonial-style atmosphere is an Oxford institution, famed
for its delectable cocktails and extensive brasserie-style menu.
Brunch is served till noon daily, afternoon tea from 14.00 to 17.30
and roast lunches on Sunday. The daily pre- and post-theatre
menus are superb value. ⓐ 5–11 Woodstock Road ☎ 01865 511995
ⓕ 01865 559042 ⓦ www.browns-restaurants.co.uk ⏱ 09.30–
23.00 Mon–Thur, 09.30–23.30 Fri & Sat, 09.30–22.30 Sun
ⓝ Bus: 6, 18, 52, 206, 853, S2, S3 (stop: Radcliffe Infirmary)

Loch Fyne Bar & Grill ££ ㉛ Tuck into the freshest of fish and
seafood dishes, served in a relaxed setting at the heart of the
trendy Jericho district. ⓐ 55 Walton Street ☎ 01865 393510
ⓦ www.lochfyne.com ⓔ oxford@lochfyne.net ⏱ 12.00–22.00
Mon–Fri, 09.00–22.30 Sat, 10.00–22.00 Sun ⓝ Bus: 17 (stop:
Juxon Street) ⓘ Children eat free at weekends and during school
holidays before 18.00

Al-Shami ££ ㉜ Hidden down a residential backstreet, this exquisite, family-run Lebanese restaurant is an absolute gem for those in the know, with its lavish tiled-and-mirrored décor, its exotic meze dishes and even Lebanese wines. It is also a favourite among Oxford's vegetarian crowd. ⓐ 25 Walton Crescent ⓣ 01865 310066 ⓦ www.al-shami.co.uk ⓔ food@al-shami.co.uk ⓛ 12.00–00.00 daily ⓝ Bus: 17 (stop: Walton Street)

Brasserie Blanc ££–£££ ㉝ Try this bright, cheery bistro, owned by local culinary giant Raymond Blanc, for a top-notch modern bistro menu served in relaxed, stylish surroundings. ⓐ 71–72 Walton Street ⓣ 01865 510999 ⓦ www.brasserieblanc.com ⓛ 12.00–14.45 & 17.30–22.00 Mon–Fri, 12.00–22.30 Sat, 12.00–21.30 Sun ⓝ Bus: 17 (Juxon Street)

AFTER DARK

Bars, pubs & live acts

The Cellar ㉞ A popular venue for alternative live music, with live music gigs and themed nights, including goth, hip-hop, electro, reggae and ska. ⓐ Frewin Court ⓣ 01865 244761 ⓦ www.cellarmusic.co.uk ⓛ Times vary with bands but typically 20.00–03.00

Duke of Cambridge ㉟ Oxford's leading cocktail bar draws a trendy, cosmopolitan crowd. ⓐ 5–6 Little Clarendon Street ⓣ 01865 558173 ⓦ www.dukebar.com ⓛ 17.00–00.00 Sun–Thur, 17.00–01.00 Fri & Sat; happy hour: 17.00–20.30 Sun–Thur, 17.00–

19.30 Fri & Sat Bus: 6, 18, 52, 206, 853, S2, S3 (stop: Radcliffe Infirmary)

The Eagle & Child ㊱ Affectionately dubbed 'The Bird & Baby', this pint-sized pub was a favourite watering-hole of C S Lewis and J R R Tolkien, who would regularly meet in the 1930s and 1940s in the cosy snugs to read their compositions aloud. ㊐ 49 St Giles ㊏ 01865 302925 ㊒ 10.00–23.00 Mon–Thur, 10.00–00.00 Fri & Sat, 10.00–22.30 Sun

Freud ㊲ This unusual bar – housed within a converted neo-classical church – is a hugely popular venue for cocktails and live jazz. ㊐ 119 Walton Street ㊏ 01865 311171 ㊍ www.freud.eu ㊎ freud.oxford@freud.eu ㊒ 20.00–late daily ㊑ Bus: 17 (stop: Walton Street)

The Jericho Tavern ㊳ Despite its somewhat shabby appearance, this is a popular locals' pub that frequently features live bands and comedy acts. ㊐ 56 Walton Street ㊏ 01865 311775 ㊍ www.thejericho.co.uk ㊒ 12.00–00.00 daily ㊑ Bus: 17 (stop: Juxon Street)

Cinema

Odeon ㊴ This national cinema chain shows all the main blockbusters in two venues. ㊐ George Street & Magdalen Street ㊏ 0871 2244007 ㊍ www.odeon.co.uk

Phoenix Picture House ㊵ A popular arthouse cinema, screening both mainstream and independent movies (including French

films on Mondays during term time). ⓐ 57 Walton Street
ⓣ 08717 042062 ⓦ www.picturehouses.co.uk
ⓔ phoenix@picturehouses.co.uk ⓒ 12.30–21.00 daily
ⓝ Bus: 17 (stop: Juxon Street)

Clubs

The Bridge ⓫ A large, sleek student disco, with cheap cocktails
and music to suit all tastes. Disco Mash Fridays is billed as 'the
best Friday night party in town'. ⓐ 6–9 Hythe Bridge Street
ⓣ 01865 242526 ⓦ www.bridgeoxford.co.uk ⓒ 21.00–02.00
Mon–Wed, 21.00–03.00 Thur, 22.00–03.00 Fri & Sat, closed Sun

Lava & Ignite ⓬ Expect to queue for this trendy nightclub, with
its vibrant choice of bars, multiple dance floors and state-of-the-
art sound and lighting. ⓐ Cantay House, Park End Street
ⓣ 01865 250181 ⓦ www.lavaignite.com ⓔ lava&ignite-
oxford@luminar.co.uk ⓒ 22.00–02.00 Mon–Thur, 22.00–03.00
Fri & Sat, closed Sun

Po Na Na ⓭ This exotic nightclub attracts a cool crowd for its
top-notch DJs and funky music mix. ⓐ 13–15 Magdalen Street
ⓣ 01865 249171 ⓦ www.oxfordponana.com ⓒ 22.00–03.00 daily

Performance arts

Ghost Trail ⓮ Join costumed, professional actor 'Bill Spectre'
outside Oxford Castle Unlocked for a spooky, spine-chilling
walking tour of Oxford's ghosts … if you dare! ⓐ Oxford Castle
Unlocked ⓣ 07941 041811 ⓦ www.ghosttrail.org
ⓔ info@ghosttrail.org ⓒ 18.30 Fri & Sat (1¼-hour tour), or join

the tour at 19.00 outside the Tourist Information Centre
📍 15–16 Broad Street (1¼-hour tour)

New Theatre 🔢 Oxford's largest theatre (formerly the Oxford Apollo) hosts everything from pantomime to opera, and musicals to ballet, including touring productions from the Welsh National Opera and Glyndebourne. 📍 George Street
📞 Box office: 0844 847 1585 🌐 www.newtheatreoxford.org.uk
🕐 Box office: 10.00–17.00 Mon–Sat (and briefly before shows)

Old Fire Station Studio 🔢 This studio-theatre-cum-gallery-cum-nightclub in a former fire station is known for its avant-garde music, theatre and dance, including student productions and experimental drama workshops from the Experimental Theatre Company. 📍 40 George Street 📞 Box office: 0844 844 0662
🌐 www.ofsstudio.org.uk; www.experimental-theatre.co.uk
🕐 Box office: 10.00–18.00 Mon–Sat, closed Sun

Oxford Playhouse 🔢 Regarded as one of Britain's leading theatres, specialising in modern drama, comedy, musicals and dance, while its intimate **Burton Taylor Studio** (named after actors Richard Burton and Elizabeth Taylor) in neighbouring Gloucester Street stages primarily experimental theatre and student productions. 📍 11–12 Beaumont Street 📞 Box office: 01865 305305 📠 01865 305335 🌐 www.oxfordplayhouse.com
🕐 Box office: 10.00–18.00 Mon–Sat (and half an hour before shows)

▶ *Blenheim Palace was Sir Winston Churchill's ancestral home and birthplace*

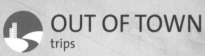

OUT OF TOWN
trips

Woodstock

Just 13 km (8 miles) north of Oxford, the historic market town of Woodstock is best known as the home of England's largest country house, Blenheim Palace. But Woodstock has more than Blenheim to offer. This fine Georgian town contains many attractive period buildings; a host of enticing shops, pubs and restaurants; a lively weekly market in the flower-clad town square; and a colourful history. Woodstock is also known as the gateway to the Oxfordshire Cotswolds, with its picturesque villages of honey-gold stone, medieval churches and green, rolling hills.

GETTING THERE

From Oxford, it takes just 20 minutes by car to Woodstock, or catch bus S3 from stop B2 (George Street) in the city centre. For further information, contact Woodstock's **Visitor Information Centre** (ⓐ Fletcher's House, Park Street ❶ 01993 813276 ⓦ www.wakeuptowoodstock.com

SIGHTS & ATTRACTIONS

Blenheim Palace
English Baroque masterpiece and World Heritage Site, Blenheim Palace is home to the Duke of Marlborough and birthplace of Sir Winston Churchill. The palace is surrounded by 850 hectares (2,100 acres) of parkland landscaped by designer 'Capability' Brown, and immaculate formal gardens. ❶ 08700 602080

ⓦ www.blenheimpalace.com ⓛ Palace and formal gardens: 10.30–17.30 daily (mid-Feb–Oct); 10.30–17.30 Wed–Sun (early Nov–mid-Dec). Park: 09.00–16.45 daily (mid-Feb–Oct); 09.00–16.45 Wed–Sun (early Nov–mid-Dec) ⓘ Admission charge

Combe Mill

See how our ancestors harnessed fire, steam and water at this fascinating working museum, in the ancient former workshop of the old Blenheim Estate. ⓐ Combe (near Long Hanborough) ⓦ www.combemill.org ⓛ 10.30–16.30 Wed & Sun; closed Mon, Tues & Thur–Sat (Mar–Oct) ⓘ Admission charge

⬤ *The sumptuous Red Drawing Room at Blenheim Palace*

Oxford Bus Museum Trust

A fascinating display of over 45 vehicles once used as public
transport in and around Oxford, from early Oxford horse trams
to old-fashioned double-decker buses. Some even offer rides
(first Sun of each month). ⓐ Station Yard, Long Hanborough
ⓘ 01993 883617 ⓦ www.oxfordbusmuseum.org.uk ⓛ 10.30–
16.30 Wed, Sat, Sun & Bank Holidays (Mar–Oct); 10.30–16.30
Wed, Sun & Bank Holidays (Nov–Feb) ⓝ Train: Hanborough
(adjacent to station) ⓘ Admission charge

Oxfordshire Cotswolds

Set at the heart of England, the Oxfordshire Cotswolds embody
all that is traditionally English: steeped in history and culture,
and rich in architectural heritage, they represent a delightful
blend of sleepy stone villages and bustling market towns,
including Witney, Burford and Chipping Norton. The Cotswolds
are also great for hiking and cycling, with an excellent network
of cycle routes and over 800 km (500 miles) of public footpaths
along meandering rivers and glorious countryside (see
ⓦ www.oxfordshirecotswolds.org for further information).

Oxfordshire Museum

This fascinating museum celebrates Oxfordshire's historical and
cultural past, with hands-on activities for all the family,
including a Jurassic garden with fossilised dinosaur footprints.
ⓐ Fletcher's House, Park Street, Woodstock ⓘ 01993 811456
ⓦ www.tomocc.org.uk ⓔ oxon.museum@oxfordshire.gov.uk
ⓛ 10.00–17.00 Tues–Sat, 14.00–17.00 Sun, closed Mon

RETAIL THERAPY

Antiques at Heritage One of several antiques shops in Woodstock, containing furniture, textiles, ceramics, paintings and collectables from 12 professional dealers. ⓐ 6 Market Place, Woodstock ⓘ 01993 811332 ⓦ www.atheritage.co.uk ⓛ 10.00–17.00 Mon–Sat, 13.00–17.00 Sun

Bluedog and Sought A cornucopia of gorgeous linens, affordable homewares, candles, ornaments and unique gift ideas, beside the church. ⓐ 5 Park Street, Woodstock ⓘ 01993 810011 ⓦ www.bluedogandsought.co.uk ⓛ 10.00–17.00 Mon–Sat, 12.00–16.00 Sun

Hampers Food and Wine Company Order a picnic hamper here for your day out at Blenheim, or create one yourself from the mouth-watering produce at this cheery deli-cum-café. ⓐ 31–33 Oxford Street, Woodstock ⓘ 01993 811535 ⓦ www.hampersfoodandwine.co.uk ⓛ 09.00–17.30 Mon–Fri, 09.00–18.00 Sat, 10.00–17.00 Sun

TAKING A BREAK

The Kings Arms ££ A mellow, contemporary brasserie, serving traditional and modern British fare in a grand Georgian townhouse. ⓐ 19 Market Street, Woodstock ⓘ 01993 813636 ⓦ www.kingshotelwoodstock.co.uk ⓛ 07.30–10.30, 12.00–14.30 & 18.30–21.30 Mon–Sat, 07.30–21.30 Sun

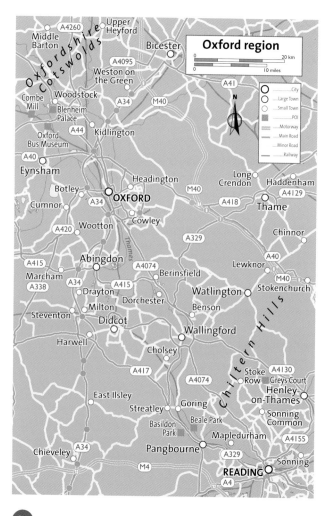

The Thames from Oxford to Henley

The Thames is a symbol of English life. It stretches 346 km
(215 miles) from the Cotswolds to London, accompanied by the
Thames Path (🌐 www.thamespath.org.uk), the only long-
distance walk to follow a river throughout its entire length.
This stretch is a popular destination, made famous by Jerome
K Jerome's travelogue *Three Men in a Boat*.

GETTING THERE

Salters Steamers (📞 01865 243421 🌐 www.salterssteamers.co.uk)
runs boat services from Oxford to Abingdon, Wallingford,
Goring, Reading, Henley and beyond (🕐 daily end May–
mid-Sept).
Buses run from Oxford to Abingdon (journey time 25 minutes)
and to Henley via Wallingford (bus X39, then bus 139; journey
time 1 hour). See 🌐 www.visitthames.co.uk for information.

SIGHTS & ATTRACTIONS

Goring

A pretty village of brick and flint cottages, with a medieval
church and excellent eateries, on the fringes of the Chiltern
Hills. Nearby **Beale Park** is a popular family outing, with its zoo,
boat trips and playgrounds. 📍 Beale Park, Lower Basildon
📞 0118 976 7498 🌐 www.goring-on-thames.co.uk,
www.bealepark.co.uk 🕐 10.00–18.00 daily (Apr–Sept); 10.00–
17.00 daily (mid-Feb–Mar & Oct) 💷 Admission charge

Henley-on-Thames

This picturesque market town is home to rowing. The **Royal Regatta** ( www.hrr.co.uk) is a world-renowned event and a great social occasion. ⓐ Tourist Office, Town Hall, Market Place ① 01491 578034 Ⓦ www.visithenley-on-thames.com

Mapledurham

Tour the last working mill on the Thames, and Mapledurham House ('Toad Hall' in *The Wind in the Willows*), with **Thames Rivercruise** (① 0118 948 1088 Ⓦ www.thamesrivercruise.co.uk). ⓐ Mill Island ① 0119 972 3350 Ⓦ www.mapledurham.co.uk ① 14.00–17.30 Sat, Sun & Bank Holidays, closed Mon–Fri (April–Sept); 1400–17.30 Sun (Oct) ① Admission charge

Pangbourne

An elegant Edwardian town of literary connections: Kenneth Grahame (author of *The Wind in the Willows*) lived here, and Jerome K Jerome and his companions finished their journey at The Swan pub in *Three Men in a Boat*.

Sonning

Known mainly for its theatre (see page 88), this charming riverside village also serves superb cream teas in the garden at **Sonning Lock** (① 11.00–17.00 daily (summer)).

Wallingford

A well-preserved market town, with a ruined castle; the impressive **Wallingford Museum** (ⓐ 52A High Street ① 01491 835065 Ⓦ www.wallingfordmuseum.org.uk); take a

steam-train ride on the **Cholsey and Wallingford Railway**
(❶ 01491 835067 Ⓦ www.cholsey-wallingford-railway.com).
ⓐ Tourist Information Centre, Town Hall, Market Place
❶ 01491 826972 Ⓦ www.wallingfordtown.co.uk

CULTURE

Stately homes include **Basildon Park**, an elegant Georgian
mansion near Pangbourne; and **Greys Court**, a fine 16th-century
mansion near Henley. Both are National Trust properties
(Ⓦ www.nationaltrust.org.uk).

River & Rowing Museum, Henley-on-Thames
A celebration of the traditions of the Thames and the sport of
rowing. ⓐ Mill Meadows, Henley-on-Thames ❶ 01491 415600
Ⓦ www.rrm.co.uk ◷ 10.00–17.30 daily (May–Aug); 10.00–17.00
daily (Sept–Apr) ❶ Admission charge

RETAIL THERAPY

Asquith's Teddy Bear Shop The world's first teddy bear shop –
crammed with bears of every size, colour and description.
ⓐ 2–4 New Street, Henley-on-Thames ❶ 01491 571978
Ⓦ www.asquiths.com ◷ 09.30–17.30 Mon–Sat, 11.00–17.00 Sun

Brightwell Vineyard Oxfordshire's largest vineyard produces
award-winning red, white, rosé and sparkling wines. ⓐ Rush
Court, Wallingford ❶ 01491 836586 Ⓦ www.brightwines.co.uk
◷ Tastings: 12.00–18.00 Fri–Sun

Jonkers Specialists in rare antiquarian books, modern first editions and illustrated children's classics. ⓐ 24 Hart Street, Henley-on-Thames ⓣ 01491 576427 ⓦ www.jonkers.co.uk ⓛ 10.00–17.30 Mon–Sat, closed Sun

TAKING A BREAK

Pierreponts £ An airy, relaxed café with an extensive menu of locally sourced produce. ⓐ High Street, Goring ⓣ 01491 874464 ⓛ 08.00–16.00 Tues–Fri, 09.00–17.00 Sat, 10.00–16.00 Sun, closed Mon

Angel on the Bridge £–££ Brilliantly located on the Thames, enjoy a hearty bar snack and a pint of locally brewed Brakesbear beer on the riverside terrace. ⓐ Thameside, Henley-on-Thames ⓣ 01491 410678 ⓦ www.theangelhenley.com ⓛ 12.00–22.00 Mon–Fri, 11.00–22.00 Sat, 12.00–19.00 Sun

Ivy of Sonning ££–£££ Sophisticated Indian cuisine. ⓐ 6 High Street, Sonning ⓣ 0118 969 7676 ⓛ 12.00–14.30 & 18.00–22.30 daily

AFTER DARK

The Mill at Sonning This riverside dinner theatre attracts leading West End actors and productions. ⓐ Sonning Eye ⓣ Box office: 0118 969 8000 ⓦ www.millatsonning.com

ⓞ *Take a sightseeing bus around Oxford*

PRACTICAL
information

Directory

GETTING THERE & AROUND
By air

Most flights from Europe and America arrive at London's two main airports, **Heathrow** (☏ 0844 335 1801 ⊛ www.heathrowairport.com) and **Gatwick** (☏ 0844 335 1802 ⊛ www.gatwickairport.com), and also at the smaller **London City Airport** (☏ 020 7646 0088 ⊛ www.londoncityairport.com) and **Birmingham International Airport** (☏ 0844 576 6000 ⊛ www.birminghamairport.co.uk). European flights also arrive at **London Stansted Airport** (☏ 0844 335 1803 ⊛ www.stanstedairport.com) and **London Luton Airport** (☏ 01582 405100 ⊛ www.london-luton.co.uk).

Oxford Bus Company operates regular bus links between Heathrow, Gatwick and Oxford (☏ 01865 785400 ⊛ www.theairline.info). **National Express** (☏ 08717 818178 ⊛ www.nationalexpress.com) runs coaches between Oxford and London Stansted Airport (journey time 3–4 hours), Luton Airport (journey time 1¼–2 hours) and Birmingham International Airport (journey time 2–4 hours).

Many people are aware that air travel emits CO_2, which contributes to climate change. You may be interested in the possibility of lessening the environmental impact of your flight through the charity **Climate Care** (⊛ www.jpmorganclimatecare.com), which offsets your CO_2 by funding environmental projects around the world.

By rail

Oxford has excellent links nationwide (National Rail Enquries ⓐ Botley Road ☎ 08457 484950 ⓦ www.nationalrail.co.uk), and a frequent service to London Paddington, run by **First Great Western** (☎ 08457 000125 ⓦ www.firstgreatwestern.co.uk). Trains to Gatwick Airport (and Brighton), Birmingham, Manchester and Scotland are provided by **CrossCountry** (☎ 0844 811 0124 ⓦ www.crosscountrytrains.co.uk).

By road

Oxford has excellent road transport links with the A34 and the M40. It is 97 km (60 miles) from London, and 113 km (70 miles) from Birmingham. There are regular coach services from London 24 hours daily (journey time approximately 1½–2 hours): the **Oxford Express** (☎ 01865 785400 ⓦ www.espress.info) runs coaches every 15–20 minutes from London's Victoria Coach Station; and the **Oxford Tube** (☎ 01865 772250 ⓦ www.oxfordtube.com) operates every 15–20 minutes from Buckingham Palace Road, near London's Victoria Railway Station.

The best option if you are arriving by car is Oxford Bus Company's highly efficient, cheap, popular **Park & Ride** scheme (☎ 01865 785400 ⓦ www.oxfordparkandride.co.uk). The car parks are located to the north at Peartree (A34/A44 junction) and Water Eaton (A4260, no Sunday service), to the west at Seacourt (A420), to the south at Redbridge (A4144), and to the east at Thornhill (A40/M40). Buses run every few minutes from early morning until early evening Monday to Saturday (Pear Tree Park & Ride service until 23.15), with a less frequent Sunday service.

HEALTH, SAFETY & CRIME

Although crime rates are low, it is advisable to take sensible precautions. **Thames Valley Police** are based at ⓐ St Aldate's, south of Christ Chur8458 505505). For emergency services (Police, Ambulance, Fire) dial ⓣ 999.

If you need to consult a doctor, ask for help at your hotel reception or call **NHS Direct** on ⓣ 0845 4647 (24 hours). The **Woodstock Road Chemist** (ⓐ 59 Woodstock Road ⓣ 01865 515226) is open 09.00–19.30 daily, including Bank Holidays. The **John Radcliffe Hospital** has an A&E unit (ⓐ Headley Way, Headington ⓣ 01865 741166 ⓦ www.oxfordradcliffe.nhs.uk).

CHILDREN

The following activities are guaranteed to appeal:

Botanic Garden: (see page 54) Family activity-backpacks appeal to all ages – choose from various themes.

City Sightseeing Bus: (see page 36) There is nothing young children like more than a ride on an open-top bus in the sunshine (while Mum and Dad enjoy the witty commentary).

G&D's: (see page 61) Luscious ice creams here (ⓐ Branches: 94 St Aldate's, 55 Little Clarendon Street and 104 Cowley Road).

Museum of the History of Science: (see page 48) Three floors of weird and wonderful scientific items.

Museum of Oxford: (see page 58) The Alice trail and brass-rubbings pack are appealing to young children.

Oxford University Museum of Natural History: (see page 49) From dodos to gigantic dinosaur skeletons, this museum is fascinating for kids of all ages.

Pitt Rivers Museum: (see page 49) Borrow a torch from the entrance desk and explore the multitude of extraordinary, unusual (and sometimes gory) exhibits hidden here.

Punting: (see page 20) Sporty children will enjoy mastering the art of punting and laughing when Mum or Dad fall in.

Science Oxford Live: A small, state-of-the-art science centre. (ⓐ 1–5 London Place ⓣ 01865 728953 ⓦ www.scienceoxford.com ⓛ 10.00–17.00 Sat (Mon–Sat during school holidays) ⓜ Bus: 7, 8, 9, 13, 15, X23 (stop: St Clements) ⓘ Admission charge).

Themed Walking Tours: The Tourist Information Centre organises a variety of walking tours (ⓦ www.visitoxford.org for details).

TRAVELLERS WITH DISABILITIES

The Tourist Information Centre provides a free booklet 'Accessible Oxford Guide', comprehensively covering provisions for the disabled. **Shopmobility** (ⓐ Level 1A, Westgate Car Park, Norfolk Street ⓣ 01865 248737) offers the free loan of wheelchairs and electric scooters for shopping and sightseeing.

Further information can be obtained from the **Oxfordshire Council of Disabled People** (ⓣ 01865 792225 ⓔ ocdp@fish.co.uk) and the **University of Oxford Disability Office** (ⓣ 01865 280459 ⓦ www.admin.ox.ac.uk/eop/disab ⓔ disability@admin.ox.ac.uk).

TOURIST INFORMATION

Get tickets for the open-top City Sightseeing bus tours and guided walks from ⓐ 15–16 Broad Street ⓣ 01865 252200 ⓦ www.visitoxford.org ⓔ tic@oxford.gov.uk ⓛ 09.30–17.00 Mon–Wed, 09.30–18.00 Thur–Sat, 10.00–16.00 Sun (July & Aug); 09.30–17.00 Mon–Sat, 10.00–16.00 Sun (Sept–June).

INDEX

ACKNOWLEDGEMENTS

The photographs in this book were taken by Karen Dexter and Kathryn West for Thomas Cook Publishing, to whom the copyright belongs, except for the following: iStockphoto pages 10 (Edyta Pawlowska), 39 (Martin Anderson), 48 (Paul Cowan), 68 (Stephen Finn).

Project editor: Tom Lee
Copy editor: Lucilla Watson
Proofreaders: Michele Greenbank & Richard Gilbert
Layout: Trevor Double
Indexer: Zoe Ross

ABOUT THE AUTHOR

Travel writer Teresa Fisher has had a love affair with Oxford ever since college days. Now, 20-plus guidebooks later, she has returned to reminisce and also to discover new facets to the ever-evolving 'city of dreaming spires'.

Send your thoughts to
books@thomascook.com

- **Found a great bar, club, shop or must-see sight that we don't feature?**
- **Like to tip us off about any information that needs a little updating?**
- **Want to tell us what you love about this handy little guidebook and more importantly how we can make it even handier?**

Then here's your chance to tell all! Send us ideas, discoveries and recommendations today and then look out for your valuable input in the next edition of this title.

Email the above address (stating the title) or write to:
pocket guides Series Editor, Thomas Cook Publishing, PO Box 227, Coningsby Road, Peterborough PE3 8SB, UK.